PRAYERS
FOR
EVERY DAY

Edited by

Rev. Victor Hoagland, C. P.

Illustrated by

Regina
Press

THE REGINA PRESS
10 Hub Drive
Melville, New York 11747

ISBN# 9780882714776

Printed in China.

TABLE OF CONTENTS

INTRODUCTION

Friend,

"Pray always." (1 Thes. 5,17) What else does this simple scriptural sentence mean except that all our lives God calls us to prayer?

Praying is not easy, as you know. Every day so many other things call for your attention. And the world around you puts little value on prayer; its advice is that you put your mind to more important matters. It is not easy to pray today.

Yet God tells you to pray.

This little book of prayers may help you. It has some short morning and evening prayers drawn from the psalms and the scriptures, some meditations for the Advent, Christmas and Lenten seasons, which are the great seasons of prayer for the church, and some selections from the word of God for your reflection.

As you use it, may the Holy Spirit within you come to your aid and guide you gently to the God who loves you.

Everyday Prayers

Sign of the Cross

In the Name of the Father, and of the Son
and of the Holy Spirit. Amen.

The Lord's Prayer

Our Father, who art in heaven,
hallowed be thy name; thy kingdom come;
thy will be done on earth as it is in heaven.
Give us this day our daily bread;
and forgive us our trespasses
as we forgive those who trespass against us;
and lead us not into temptation,
but deliver us from evil.

The Hail Mary

Hail, Mary, full of grace,
the Lord is with you.
Blessed are you among women,
and blessed is the fruit of your womb, Jesus.
Holy Mary Mother of God,
pray for us sinners,
now and at the hour of our death. Amen.

The Doxology

Glory be to the Father, and to the Son, and to the Holy Spirit; as it was in the beginning, is now, and will be forever. Amen.

The Apostle's Creed

I believe in God, the Father almighty, creator of heaven and earth. I believe in Jesus Christ, His only Son, our Lord.

He was conceived by the power of the Holy Spirit and born of the Virgin Mary. He suffered under Pontius Pilate, was crucified, died, and was buried. He descended to the dead. On the third day He rose again. He ascended into heaven, and is seated at the right hand of the Father. He will come again to judge the living and the dead.

I believe in the Holy Spirit, the holy catholic Church, the communion of saints, the forgiveness of sins, the resurrection of the body, and the life everlasting. Amen.

PRAYERS FOR MORNING AND EVENING

SUNDAY MORNING

O God, You are my God,
for You I long;
for You my soul is thirsting.
I long for You
like dry, weary land
without water.
Give me Your strength
and Your glory.

I wish to praise You all my life;
fill my soul as with a banquet.
I cling to You;
hold me close in Your hands.

Psalm 63

Glory be to the Father…

READING

Jesus said,

"Whoever drinks the water I give will never be thirsty; no, the water I give shall become a fountain within him, leaping up to provide eternal life." The woman said to Him, "Give me this water, Sir, so that I shall not grow thirsty"…

Jn 4:14-15

INTERCESSIONS

Blessed are you, Lord Jesus, Savior of the world, for giving Your life to save us,
— by Your precious blood we are saved.

You promised living waters to those who seek the truth,
— give us that water to quench our thirst.

You sent disciples to announce the Good News to all people,
— sustain those who proclaim Your word.

To those who carry Your Cross today in anguish,
— grant patience and courage.

SUNDAY EVENING

The Lord is my shepherd;
I shall not want.
In verdant pastures
He gives me repose.
Beside restful waters
He leads me;
He refreshes my soul.
He guides me in right paths
for His name's sake.
Even though I walk in the dark valley
I fear no evil;
for You are at my side
with Your rod and Your staff
that give me courage.
You spread the table before me
in the sight of my foes;
You anoint my head with oil;
my cup overflows.
Only goodness and kindness
follow me all the days of my life;
and I shall dwell in the house of the Lord
for years to come.

Psalm 23

Glory be to the Father…

READING

Jesus said,

"I am the good shepherd, I know my sheep
and my sheep know Me in the same way
that the Father knows Me and I know My
Father; for these sheep I will give My life."

John 10:14-15

INTERCESSIONS

We bless You, Jesus Christ, our Shepherd,
for the life You have given us this day.
— we rejoice in Your love.

Look with favor on the flock that bears
Your name,
— let no one the Father has given
    You perish.

Guide Your church in the way of Your Truth,
— by Your Holy Spirit make her faithful.

Feed us at the table of Your Word and
Your Bread,
— that we may follow You forever.

MONDAY MORNING

I call upon You, O Lord.
In the morning You hear me;
In the morning
I offer you my prayer,
watching and waiting…

Psalm 5

I lift my heart to You, O Lord,
to be strengthened for this day.
Be with me in all I do, my God;
guide me in all my ways.

I will carry some burdens today;
some trials will be mine.
So I wait for Your help, Lord,
lest I stumble and fall.

I will do my work, Father,
the work begun by Your Son.
He lives in me and I in Him;
may His work today be done.

Glory be to the Father…

Reading

Do to no one what you yourself dislike. Give to the hungry some of your bread, and to the naked some of your clothing. Seek counsel from every wise person. At all times bless the Lord God, and ask God to make all your paths straight; and to grant success to all your endeavors and plans.

Tobit 4:15a, 16a, 18a, 19

Intercessions

God of all kindness, bless Your church
— make Your people faithful to You.

Eternal Shepherd, look kindly on our Holy Father and all bishops,
— grant them wisdom and courage.

Ruler of Nations, look kindly on these who govern,
— guide them in the ways of peace.

Judge of the living and the dead, be merciful to our deceased brothers and sisters,
— receive them into eternal joy.

Monday Evening

Father in heaven,
I lift my eyes to You
and wait for Your help.
I am Your servant,
entrusted with Your gifts;
I am Yours alone.

I lift my eyes to You
who dwell in heaven.
Like a faithful servant, I wish
to do Your bidding.

As the eyes of a good servant
are on the master,
So are our eyes on the Lord,
our God, till He bless us.

Psalm 12

Glory be to the Father…

READING

See what love the Father
has bestowed on us
in letting us be called children of God!

Yes that is what we are.

Dearly beloved,
we are God's children now;
what we shall later be has not yet
come to light.
We know that when it comes to light
we shall be like Him as He is.

1 John 3:1a-2

INTERCESSIONS

Lord, remember Your church throughout
the world,
— that Your people may dwell in peace.

Lord, remember those we have met today,
— that they may receive Your gifts.

Lord, remember all families
— that they may live in harmony.

Lord, remember the sick and the dying,
— that they may have Your joy.

TUESDAY MORNING

Lord, teach us to
number our days aright,
that we may gain
wisdom of heart…

Psalm 90

Help us do today
the things that matter,
not to waste the time we have.

Yes, the moments we have
are precious, Lord,
see that we count them dear.
Teach us to
number our days aright.
Fill us this day
with Your kindness,
that we may be glad and rejoice
all the days of our life.

Glory be to the Father…

READING

What we await are new heavens and a new earth where, according to his promise, the justice of God will reside. So, beloved, while waiting for this, make every effort to be found without stain or defilement, and at peace in His sight. Consider that our Lord's patience is directed toward salvation.

2 Peter 3:13-15a

INTERCESSION

Christ, our Guide, grant that today we may follow what You command,
— we humbly ask You.

Christ, our Guide, grant that today Your life may grow within us,
— we humbly ask You.

Christ, our Guide, grant that today we may live in peace,
— we humbly ask You.

Christ, our Guide, grant that today we may not fall into sin,
— we humbly ask You.

TUESDAY EVENING

Lord, as this day ends,
soul and body, I am tired.
And all I have done:
is it worthwhile?
I need You, Lord,
where can I turn,
except to You?

O Lord, my heart is not proud,
nor are my eyes haughty;
I busy not myself with great things
too sublime for me.
Nay rather, I have stilled
and quieted
my soul like a weaned child.
Like a weaned child
on its mothers lap,
so is my soul within me.
O Israel, hope in the Lord,
both now and forever.

Psalm 131

Glory be to the Father…

Reading

Praised be God, the Father of our Lord Jesus Christ, the Father of mercies and the God of all consolation! He comforts us in all our afflictions and thus enables us to comfort those who are in trouble, with the same consolation we have received from Him.

2 Corinthians 1:3-4

Intercessions

Lord Jesus, intercede for us with Your heavenly Father,
— despite our offenses, abide with us.

Lord Jesus, conqueror of death, strengthen our faith in Your resurrection,
— in the stillness of night, abide with us.

Lord Jesus, image of the unseen God, help us to know the Father,
— in our works, abide with us.

Lord Jesus, light of the world, bring us hope that never fails,
— by Your Spirit, abide with us.

WEDNESDAY MORNING

Praise the Lord, O my soul.
I will praise the Lord all my life;
I will sing praise to my God
while I live…

Psalm 146

Praise the Lord,
my mind and memory,
my thoughts and deeds
of this day.
I will praise the Lord
wherever I go;
I will sing praise,
for the Lord is good.

Praise the Lord,
strangers and friends;
let us praise Him for He loves us;
let us sing praise to our God
while we live.

Glory be to the Father…

READING

Love is patient; love is kind. Love is not
jealous, it does not put on airs, it is not
snobbish. Love is never rude, it is not self-
seeking, it is not prone to anger; neither does
it brood over injuries. Love does not rejoice
in what is wrong but rejoices with the truth.
There is no limit to love's forbearance, to its
trust, its hope, its power to endure.

1 Corinthians 13:4-7

INTERCESSIONS

Blessed are you, Creator of heaven and
earth,
— You made the world and offer it life.

Remember us as we begin our work,
— that we work in harmony with others.

May we do what is useful for our brothers
and sisters,
— and together build a world that is
  pleasing to You.

To us and all whom we meet today,
— give Your joy and peace.

WEDNESDAY EVENING

The Lord is my light
and my salvation,
whom should I fear?
The Lord is my life's refuge;
of whom should I be afraid?

One thing I ask of the Lord;
this I seek:
To dwell in the house of the Lord
all the days of my life.
That I may gaze
on the loveliness of the Lord
and contemplate His temple.

Here, O Lord,
the sound of my call;
have pity on me, and answer me.
Of You my heart speaks;
You my glance seeks;
Your presence, O Lord, I seek.

Psalm 27

Glory be to the Father...

READING

May the Lord increase you and make you overflow with love for one another and for all, even as our love does for you. May He strengthen your hearts, making them blameless and holy before our God and Father at the coming of our Lord Jesus Christ with all His holy ones.

1 Thessalonians 3:12-13

INTERCESSIONS

Jesus, our Savior, from Your pierced heart the church was born,
— by Your holy Cross give us new life.

Jesus, our Savior, the centurion proclaimed You were God's Son,
— by Your holy Cross increase our faith.

Jesus, our Savior, You called the good thief into paradise,
— by Your holy Cross, call us.

Jesus, our Savior, You cured the sick and raised the dead,
— by Your holy Cross, save us.

Thursday Morning

Sing joyfully to the Lord,
all you lands;
serve the Lord with gladness;
come before Him
with joyful song.
Know that the Lord is God;
He made us, His we are;
His people, the flock He tends.
Enter His gates
with thanksgiving,
His courts with praise;
Give thanks to Him;
bless His name, for
He is good:
the Lord,
whose kindness endures forever,
and His faithfulness
to all generations.

Psalm 100

Glory be to the Father…

Reading

All of you should be like-minded, sympathetic, loving toward one another, kindly disposed, and humble. Do not return evil for evil or insult for insult. Return a blessing instead. This you have been called to do, that you may receive a blessing as your inheritance.

1 Peter 3:8-9

Intercessions

Lord, our refuge and strength, listen to our praise at the beginning of this day,
— teach us to praise You without end.

In You we place our faith and hope,
— that our waiting might be rewarded.

You know our needs and come to our aid,
— without You we can do nothing.

Remember the poor and unfortunate,
— may this day not be a burden to them.

THURSDAY EVENING

Lord, I thank You
for the many times
You gave me help,
always listening when I called.

In my darkest moments,
when all seemed to be lost,
there You were, at my side.

The Lord always listens
and has pity;
the Lord always
comes to our help.

Our mourning You change
into dancing;
You always clothe us with joy.

So my soul sings praise
to you unceasingly.
O Lord my God,
I will thank You forever.

Psalm 30

Glory be to the Father…

READING

There is cause for rejoicing here. You may for a time have to suffer the distress of many trials; but this is so that your faith, which is more precious than the passing splendor of fire-tried gold, may by its genuineness lead to praise, glory, and honor when Jesus Christ appears. Although you have never seen Him, you love Him, and without seeing you now believe in Him, and rejoice with inexpressible joy touched with glory because you are achieving faith's goal, your salvation.   1 Peter 1:6-9

INTERCESSIONS

We praise you, God our Father, for the life You give us today,
— blessed are You, O Lord.

We praise You for Your Son who fills us with wisdom and knowledge,
— blessed are You, O Lord.

We praise You, Father of mercies, for preserving us from temptation,
— blessed are You, O Lord.

We praise You, God of kindness, for giving strength to the weak,
— blessed are You, O Lord.

Friday Morning

Have mercy on me, O God,
in Your goodness;
in the greatness
of Your compassion
wipe out my offense.
Thoroughly wash me
from my guilt
and of my sin cleanse me.
A clean heart create for me,
O God,
and a steadfast spirit
renew within me.
Cast me not out from Your presence,
and Your Holy Spirit
take not from me.
Cleanse me of sin with hyssop,
that I may be purified;
wash me, and I shall be whiter than snow.
Let me hear the sounds
of joy and gladness;
the bones you have crushed shall rejoice.

Psalm 51

Glory be to the Father…

READING

Never let evil talk pass your lips; say only the good things people need to hear, things that will really help them. Do nothing that will sadden the Holy Spirit with whom you were sealed against the day of redemption. Get rid of all bitterness, all passion and anger, harsh words, slander, and malice of every kind. In place of these, be kind to one another, compassionate, and mutually forgiving, just as God has forgiven you in Christ.

Ephesians 4:29-32

INTERCESSIONS

We give You thanks, Lord, for You are rich in mercy,
— for the great love with which You have loved us.

You are acting always in the world by the power of Your Spirit,
— making all things new.

Open our eyes today, and those of our brothers and sisters
— that we may see Your wonders.

My God, every day I praise You,
my voice blending
with the prayer
of every generation.

You are good and merciful,
slow to anger
and of great kindness.
The Lord is faithful
in all His words
and holy in all His works.
The Lord lifts up
all who are falling
and raises up
all who are bowed down.
The eyes of all look
hopefully to You,
and You give them their food
in due season;
You open Your hand
and satisfy the desire
of every living thing.

Psalm 145

Glory be to the Father…

READING

Who will separate us from the love of
Christ? Trial, or distress, or persecution,
or hunger, or nakedness, or danger,
or the sword? Yet in all this we are more
than conquerors because of Him who has
loved us.

Romans 8:35-37

INTERCESSIONS

Jesus, who died on the Cross for us, forgive
the sins we have committed this day,
— Lord, hear us! Lord, help us!

Jesus, conqueror of death, take our deceased
brothers and sisters with You into paradise,
— Lord, hear us! Lord, help us!

Jesus, born of Mary, give us a readiness like
hers to welcome Your word,
— Lord, hear us! Lord, help us!

SATURDAY MORNING

Praise the Lord, all you nations,
glorify God, all you peoples!
For steadfast is God's kindness
toward us
and the fidelity of the Lord
endures forever...

Psalm 117

Praise the Lord, faraway space,
glorify God,
every home and family!
For God has brought us
to the beginning of this day,
and God will see us to its end.

Praise the Lord, world of today,
come with Your blessings;
come with Your struggles.

Praise the Lord!

Glory be to the Father...

READING

May God, the source of all patience and encouragement, enable you to live in perfect harmony with one another according to the spirit of Christ Jesus, so that with one heart and voice you may glorify God, the Father of our Lord Jesus Christ. Accept one another, then, as Christ accepted you, for the glory of God.   Romans 15:5-7

INTERCESSIONS

O God, You are our blessed light,
— awaken us this new day.

By the resurrection of Your Son, You have enlightened the world,
— and given us new hope.

By Your Spirit, You gave wisdom to the disciples of Your Son,
— send Your Spirit upon us and make us faithful.

Light of the nations, shine on those who dwell in darkness,
— open their eyes to know You, the only true God.

SATURDAY EVENING

Out of the depths I cry to You,
Lord, hear my voice…

Psalm 130

From my fears, failures and sins,
I cry to You.
Lord, hear my voice.

From the depths of my heart
I cry to You,
from the darkness of myself.
From life's shadow I cry to You.
Lord, hear my voice.

For You are merciful, Lord,
forgiving to us all.
And so I wait, Lord,
Your mercy comes
as sure as the dawn.

Glory be to the Father…

READING

More tortuous than all else is the human heart, beyond remedy; who can understand it?

I, the Lord, alone probe the mind
and test the heart,
To reward everyone according to his ways,
according to the merit of his deeds.

Jeremiah 17:9-10

INTERCESSIONS

O God, blessed through all ages,
You guide us always with Your light,
— we praise You through Jesus Christ.

O God, blessed through all ages,
You nourish us with daily bread,
— we praise You through Jesus Christ.

O God, blessed through all ages, You
strengthen us with Your powerful grace,
— we praise You through Jesus Christ.

God of Glory, blessed through all ages glorify
those who love You,
— we praise You through Jesus Christ.

Prayers for Advent and Christmas Season

First Week of Advent

"Jesus said to his disciples: 'Be constantly on the watch! Stay awake!…You do not know when the Master of the house is coming.'"

Mk. 13:33

O Jesus, Your voice sounds through the house of my world: Be on Your guard! Stay awake!

Yet I hardly hear You. Busy with so much, I go about the things I do like a servant trapped in household routine, hardly giving a thought to what my life is about. My spirit within has grown tired and You, my God, seem far away. How can I hear Your voice today?

Speak to my heart during this season of grace, as You spoke to Your prophets and saints. Remind me again of the journey You call me to make and the work You would have me do. I am Your servant, O Lord. Speak to me in this holy season and turn my eyes to watch for Your coming.

O Emmanuel, Jesus Christ, desire of every nation, Savior of all peoples, come and dwell among us.

"When John the Baptizer made his appearance as a preacher in the desert of Judea, this was his theme: Reform your lives. The reign of God is at hand!"

Mt. 3:1

O Jesus, in an empty desert Your prophet John proclaimed: God is here, at your side. God has come to bring about a kingdom where injustice and suffering will be no more, where tears will be wiped away, and where those who turn to God will feast at a banquet.

"Turn now, Your God is standing at Your side. Reform Your lives, God's kingdom is at hand." In an empty desert John said these things.

Give me faith like John's, O Lord, strong enough to believe even in a desert that You and Your kingdom are no farther from me than my hand. Make my heart strong like his, not swayed by trials or snared by false pleasures. Give me courage to be faithful until Your promises are fulfilled.

O King of all nations, Jesus Christ, only joy of every heart, come and save Your people.

Third Week of Advent

John's disciples said to Jesus, "Are You 'He who is to come' or do we look for another?" In reply, Jesus said: "Tell John what you hear and see: the blind recover their sight, cripples walk, lepers are cured, and the poor have good news preached to them…"

Lk. 3:10

O Jesus, I rejoice at the signs that say You are near. Your power is everywhere if I could see it.

Yet my eyes often see only darkness and what has yet to be done. I believe in You, yet when I look around evil seems so strong and goodness so weak. If You have come, why is there still so much suffering and why do the poor still despair? Where are Your miracles today?

Your grace, O Lord, is more fruitful in my world than I imagine. I know Your power is everywhere around me, if I could only see it. Show me today where the blind see and cripples walk.

Make my vision sharper than it is.

The angel Gabriel said to Mary, "Do not fear, Mary, you shall conceive and bear a son and give Him the name Jesus. Great will be His dignity and He will be called Son of the Most High…"

Lk. 1

O Jesus, I believe You were born of Mary and are God's Son.

Your mysterious coming is beyond understanding. Yet like Your holy mother, Mary, I wish that You come to me, for You promised You will. Let me serve You in any way I can and know that You are with me day by day as my life goes by.

Like Mary, Your mother, though I know You only by faith, may my whole being proclaim Your greatness and my spirit rejoice in Your favor to me.

O Wisdom, holy Word of God, Jesus Christ, holding all things in Your strong yet tender hands, come and show us the way to salvation.

A READING FROM THE HOLY GOSPEL
ACCORDING TO LUKE

In those days Caesar Augustus published a decree ordering a census of the whole world.

This first census took place while Quirinius was governor of Syria. Everyone went to register, each to his own town.

And so Joseph went from the town of Nazareth in Galilee to Judea, to David's town of Bethlehem — because he was of the house and lineage of David — to register with Mary, his espoused wife, who was with child.

While they were there the days of her confinement were completed. She gave birth to her first-born son and wrapped Him in swaddling clothes and laid Him in a manger, because there was no room for them in the place where travelers lodged.

There were shepherds in the locality,
living in the fields and keeping night watch
by turns over their flock.
The angel of the Lord appeared to them,
as the glory of the Lord shone around them,
and they were very much afraid.
The angel said to them:
"You have nothing to fear!
I come to proclaim good news to you —
tidings of great joy to be shared by the
whole people.
This day in David's city a savior
has been born to you, the Messiah and Lord.
Let this be a sign to you:
in a manger you will find an infant
wrapped in swaddling clothes."
Suddenly, there was with the angel
a multitude of the heavenly host,
praising God and saying,
"Glory to God in high heaven,
peace on earth to those on whom
His favor rests."

Luke 2: 1-14

This is the Gospel of the Lord.

PRAYERS TO MARY, THE MOTHER OF GOD

THE HAIL MARY

Hail Mary, full of grace,
the Lord is with you!
Blessed are you among women,
and blessed is the fruit of your womb, Jesus.
Holy Mary, Mother of God,
pray for us sinners,
now and at the hour of our death.
Amen.

THE REGINA CAELI
"QUEEN OF HEAVEN"

Queen of heaven, rejoice, Alleluia.
The Son whom you were privileged to bear,
Alleluia, has risen as he said, Alleluia.

Pray to God for us, Alleluia.

Rejoice and be glad, Virgin Mary, Alleluia.
For the Lord has truly risen. Alleluia.

Let us pray. O God
it was by the Resurrection of your Son,

our Lord Jesus Christ,
that you brought joy to the world.

Grant that through the intercession of the Virgin
Mary, his Mother, we may attain the joy of
eternal life.

Through Christ, our Lord. Amen.

THE MEMORARE

Remember, O most gracious Virgin Mary,
that never was it known that
anyone who fled to your protection,
implored your help,
or sought your intercession
was left unaided.

Inspired by this confidence, we fly unto you, O
Virgin of virgins, our Mother!

To you we come, before you we stand,
sinful and sorrowful.

O Mother of the Word incarnate,
despise not our petitions, but
in your mercy hear and answer us.
Amen.

THE ANGELUS

The angel of the Lord declared unto Mary.

And she conceived of the Holy Spirit.

> Hail Mary…

Behold the handmaid of the Lord.

Be it done to me according to your word.

> Hail Mary…

And the Word was made flesh;
and dwelt among us. Hail Mary…

Pray for us, O holy Mother of God, that we may
be made worthy of the promises of Christ.

Let us pray.
Pour forth, we beseech you, O Lord, your grace
in our hearts, that we, to whom the Incarnation
of Christ, your Son, was made known
by the message of an angel,
may by his passion and cross
be brought to the glory of his resurrection;
through the same Christ our Lord.
Amen.

THE STATIONS
OF THE CROSS

The Stations of the Cross is an ancient devotion for meditating on the Passion of Jesus. Remembering the final hours of our Savior as they are related in the gospels and tradition, we know better what Jesus meant when He said, "Take up your cross and follow Me."

In memory and imagination, take your place along the way that Jesus walked. With Mary and the holy women, stand watching and consider in faith God's only Son, who loved us and died for us.

O Mother of my Savior,
You stand beside your Son.
With love beyond all telling,
You share His grief as one.
How shall I know your sorrow,
Your tears beyond compare?
Deep in my heart stand watching,
And call my memory there.

Lord Jesus Christ,
I come in faith to remember Your
passion and death.
Let me walk at Your side during Your
last journey.
Open my mind and touch my heart
that I may understand how deep is the love
You showed us in Your final hours.
As I remember Your sorrows,
let me see too the sufferings others bear.
Make me know the cross my neighbor
carries as I gaze on Yours.

O my God,
inspire me to follow bravely in Your steps,
carrying my own cross after You.
Long ago the prophet spoke these words
for You:

"The Lord God has given me a well trained
tongue, that I might know how to speak to the
weary a word that will rouse them"(Is. 50:4).
Speak to me, Lord, from Your wounds and
Your sufferings.
Stir my tired spirit to love You.

FIRST STATION

JESUS IS CONDEMNED TO DEATH

Pilate brought Jesus outside and said to the people, "Look at your king!" At this they shouted, "Away with Him! Crucify Him!" Then Pilate handed Jesus over to be crucified.

MEDITATION

Lord Jesus Christ, I believe you are my King, I wish for no other. Though You stand silently in chains, You are God, the Word through whom all things were made, the Savior sent to redeem us.

As I make my decisions and judgments in life, let me remember this scene of Your judgment. Give me a sense of true values, lest I betray what is right, and so betray You.

Guide the choices I make,
however hard they may be,
my King and my judge.

The Lord is near to all who call on Him.

Second Station

Jesus Carries His Cross

Jesus was led away, and carrying the Cross
by Himself, went out to what is called the
Place of the Skull, Golgotha.

Meditation

Lord Jesus Christ,
what a strange gift we give You, this Cross!

How different from the gifts You bring to us,
comfort, healing, encouragement.
Now here is our repayment, a Cross!

My own return is there also
in that painful burden You bear.
I have been ungrateful for Your love.

Lord, I see You still holding and carrying a
sinful world in this Cross of Yours.
Take me, Lord, sinful and coarse,
and refine my life,
through Your redeeming love.

O God, You are my helper, give me strength.

THIRD STATION

JESUS FALLS THE FIRST TIME

Jesus emptied Himself, and took the form of
a slave, being born in the likeness of men.
He humbled Himself, to death and a Cross.

MEDITATION

Lord Jesus Christ,
how strange a sight to see You,
our Mighty God, stumble and fall.
Weakened by Your sufferings
and the weight of the Cross,
You fall as all men and women do,
when they reach the end of their strength.

Lord, remember the empty taste
of Your own weakness,
and be with me when I cannot go on.
You are my hope and my strength,
my rock and my shield.
When I reach the limit of my endurance,
when my heart and body fail,
be with me at my side.

The Lord is Rock, and He is my salvation.

FOURTH STATION

JESUS MEETS HIS MOTHER

Simeon said to Mary, His mother: "This child is destined to be the downfall and the rise of many in Israel, a sign that will be opposed. And you yourself shall be pierced with a sword, so that the thoughts of many hearts will be laid bare."

MEDITATION

Lord Jesus Christ, Your meeting with Your mother here on the way to Calvary is the sword that Simeon foretold would pierce her heart.

To her, You are not an unfortunate man on the way to His death. You are her Son. She bore You in a stable; she watched You grow in wisdom and grace, she took pride in Your public life. Now she must share in the anguish of Your death.

Lord, may I share in Your mysteries together with Your mother. And as I share with You, may You share in all the events of my life, in my joys, my achievements, my sorrows.

I mourn with you, O Mary, Mother of God.

FIFTH STATION

SIMON OF CYRENE HELPS JESUS BEAR HIS CROSS

A man named Simon of Cyrene, was coming in from the fields, and they pressed him into service to carry the Cross.

MEDITATION

Lord Jesus Christ, unlike Your mother, Simon of Cyrene was a passing stranger, unready and unwilling to share his life with You, particularly when it meant the social disgrace of carrying Your Cross. Did he come to see You as the Light of the World under Your guise of sorrow? All men and women are meant to.

Lord, in all places and situations where You offer to share Your Cross with me, may I remember that the Cross is Yours and You are asking me to share in the glory of it. Help me to take it up willingly.

I shall not want; my shepherd is the Lord.

Sixth Station

Veronica Wipes The Face Of Jesus

He who welcomes you, welcomes Me; and he who welcomes Me, welcomes Him who sent Me. And I promise that whoever gives a cup of cold water will not want for his reward.

Meditation

Lord Jesus Christ,
in compassion Veronica offered You a towel
to wipe the dust and blood and sweat from
Your face.
She dared the contempt and hostility
of an excited crowd,
for, under Your disfigurement,
she discerned the glory of the Son of God.

Lord,
in the needy and unnoticed
people of this world,
may I see Your face
and open my heart to them.

I seek Your face, O Lord, and I shall live.

SEVENTH STATION

JESUS FALLS THE SECOND TIME

But I am a worm, not a man; the scorn of men, despised of the people. All who see me scoff at me.

MEDITATION

Lord Jesus Christ,
in Your miracles You healed the blind,
the lepers, those who were paralyzed.
Now in Your passion You experience
their darkness,
their misery, their helplessness.
Falling beneath your Cross,
You feel the depths of all human sorrow.

Lord,
may I not run away from human misery
in others and in myself.
Following in Your steps,
let me heal when I can
and suffer patiently when I cannot.

O God, make haste to help me in my need.

EIGHTH STATION

JESUS SPEAKS TO THE WOMEN OF JERUSALEM

A great crowd of people followed him, including women who beat their breasts and lamented over Him. Jesus turned to them and said: "Daughters of Jerusalem, do not weep over Me. Weep for yourselves and for your children."

MEDITATION

Lord Jesus Christ, how surprising to see You from the depths of Your sorrow reach out and give! Meeting the sorrowing women, You think less of Yourself than of them. "Weep not for Me, but for your children." Your Passion is truly a pouring out of Yourself for others!

Lord, may my own troubles and sufferings not make me unmindful of my neighbor's needs. Let me support others and give, even when I myself am in sorrow.

A humble heart, O God, I offer you.

NINTH STATION

JESUS FALLS THE THIRD TIME

I am like water poured out; all my bones are racked. You have brought me down to the dust of death.

MEDITATION

Lord Jesus Christ,
You refuse to use Your godly power
to prevent Your falling a third time.
You lie there helpless,
abandoned even by Your disciples.
You had commanded the wind and the sea
but now you have no strength
to lift Yourself to Your feet.

Lord, in my strength,
let me be aware of my weakness.
In my weakness,
let me have the support of that power
which You refused to use for Yourself.
You do not abandon the poor
who hope in Your kindness.

O wait, be strong; O wait before the Lord.

TENTH STATION

JESUS IS STRIPPED OF HIS GARMENTS

They stripped off His clothes and began to mock Him saying: "All hail, King of the Jews!"

MEDITATION

Lord Jesus Christ, now You suffer this new indignity when the soldiers strip You of Your garments. As Son of Man with no place to lay Your head, You accepted the poverty of a manger and a homeless public life.

Now Your very clothing is taken from You and You are shamed in the eyes of men. Emptying Yourself of all You possessed, You fulfill Your Father's plan for the coming of His kingdom.

Lord, seeing You stripped of your garments, may I repeat with the prophet Job: "Naked I came forth from my mother's womb and naked shall I go back again. The Lord gave and the Lord has taken away, blessed be the name of the Lord."

I trust in God, I shall not be ashamed.

ELEVENTH STATION

JESUS IS NAILED TO THE CROSS

After carrying His Cross, Jesus came to the Place of the Skull (in Hebrew, Golgotha). There they crucified Him and two others with Him.

MEDITATION

Lord Jesus Christ, nailed to the Cross and immobilized, Your suffering typifies that which comes to everyone who experiences life's harsh limitations.

You know the sorrow of everyone bound by poor health, by what they might call bad luck, by family tragedy, by opposition, by years and years of getting nowhere.

Lord, as I feel such nails limiting my hopes and expectations, as I experience the Cross which binds me to what seems like futility, give me some of Your patience to transform what I endure.

To You, O Lord, I lift my soul in prayer.

TWELFTH STATION

JESUS DIES ON THE CROSS

Jesus said, "I thirst!" and they gave him
wine. "It is finished!" He cried, and gave up
His spirit.

MEDITATION

Lord Jesus Christ,
You open Your arms on the Cross
and lovingly embrace a sinful world.
You are the Word, through whom all things
were made.

You are the Life whose death renews
everything. You are the Holy One who takes
upon Yourself the sins of us all. You wash the
earth clean by Your precious Blood. All men
and women from the time of Adam
surround Your life-giving Cross and praise
Your infinite love.

Lord, I stand beneath Your Cross, my arms
open, to thank You for offering Your life for
me.

I shall not die, O Lord, but I shall live.

THIRTEENTH STATION

JESUS IS TAKEN DOWN FROM THE CROSS

When the soldiers came to Jesus and saw that He was already dead, they did not break His legs. But one of the soldiers thrust a lance into His side, and blood and water flowed out. Thus was the Scripture fulfilled: "They shall look on Him whom they have pierced."

MEDITATION

Lord Jesus Christ,
You empty Yourself
accepting death
even on a Cross.
Obedient to the Father,
You trust in His goodness
even to the test of death.

Lord, give me an unfailing trust in Your love for me. Let my last breath commend my spirit into the Father's hands.

The stone cast off becomes the cornerstone.

Fourteenth Station

Jesus Is Laid In The Tomb

Joseph of Arimathea asked Pilate for the body of Jesus, and wrapped it in perfumed oils. Then he buried Jesus in a tomb close at hand.

Meditation

Lord Jesus,
Your friends carry Your body for burial
to a tomb in a garden.
But You will break the bonds of death
and bless every tomb
with the power and hope of Resurrection.

Lord, make me rise again
after dying with You.
May all those who have fallen asleep
rise again.

I rest in hope. I shall arise from sleep.

A Reading from the Holy Gospel According to Matthew

After the sabbath, as the first day of the week was dawning, Mary Magdalene came with the other Mary to inspect the tomb.

Suddenly there was a mighty earthquake, as the angel of the Lord descended from heaven. He came to the stone, rolled it back, and sat on it.

In appearance he resembled a flash of lightning while his garments were as dazzling as snow. The guards grew paralyzed with fear of him and fell down like dead men.

Then the angel spoke, addressing the women: "Do not be frightened. I know you are looking for Jesus the crucified, but He is not here. He has been raised, exactly as He promised.

Come and see the spot where He was laid.
Then go quickly and tell His disciples:
'He has been raised from the dead
and now goes ahead of you to Galilee,
where you will see Him.'
That is the message I have for you."

They hurried away from the tomb
half-overjoyed, half-fearful, and ran to carry
the good news to His disciples.

Suddenly, without warning, Jesus stood
before them and said, "Peace!"
The women came up and embraced His feet
and did Him homage. At this Jesus said to
them, "Do not be afraid! Go and carry the
news to My brothers that they are to go to
Galilee, where they will see Me."

Matthew 28: 1-10

This is the Gospel of the Lord.

THOUGHTS FROM HOLY SCRIPTURE

THE GIFT OF LOVE

God so loved the world
that He sent His only Son,
so that everyone who believes in Him
might not perish
but might have eternal life.

Jn. 3:16

You shall love the Lord, your God,
with all your heart, and with all your soul,
and with all your mind.
This is the greatest and
the first commandment.
The second is like it:
You shall love your neighbor as yourself.

Mt. 22:37-39

Love one another.
As I have loved you,
so you also should love one another.

Jn. 13:34

If I speak in human and angelic tongues
but do not have love,
I am a resounding gong
or a clashing cymbal.
And if I have the gift of prophecy
and comprehend all mysteries
and all knowledge;
if I have all faith so as to move mountains
but do not have love, I am nothing.
If I give away everything I own,
and if I hand my body over
so that I may boast but do not have love,
I gain nothing.
Love is patient, love is kind.
It is not jealous, love is not pompous,
it is not inflated, it is not rude,
it does not seek its own interests,
it is not quick-tempered,
it does not brood over injury,
it does not rejoice over wrongdoing
but rejoices with the truth.
It bears all things, believes all things,
hopes all things, endures all things.

1 Cor. 13:1-7

Everything Has Its Time

There is a time for everything,
a time for every purpose under heaven.
A time to be born, and a time to die;
a time to plant,
and a time to uproot the plant.
A time to kill, and a time to heal;
a time to tear down and a time to build.
A time to weep, and a time to laugh;
a time to mourn, and a time to dance.
A time to scatter stones,
and a time to gather them;
A time to embrace,
and a time to be far from embracing.
A time to seek, and a time to lose;
a time to keep, and a time to cast away.
A time to mend, and a time to sew;
a time to be silent, and a time to speak.
A time to love, and a time to hate;
a time of war, and a time of peace.

Eccles. 3:1-8

HOW TO LIVE YOUR LIFE

Entrust your work to God
and your plans will succeed.

Prov. 16:3

What you can do, do.
You can do nothing about what is
beyond you.

Sir. 3:21

Walk with the wise and you will be wise, if
you go with fools you will fall.

Prov. 13:30

As one face differs from another
so does one human heart from another.

Prov. 27-19

Never say no to truth
you will struggle against a rushing stream.

Sir. 4:25

Train your children
in the way they should go,
even when they are old
they will not swerve from it.

Prov. 22:6

A gentle tongue is a tree of life.

Prov. 1 5:4

Anyone who is kind to the poor lends to
God, and God will repay the deed.

Prov. 19:17

GOD ANSWERS OUR PRAYERS

Ask and it will be given to you;
seek and you will find;
knock and the door will be opened to you.
For everyone who asks, receives;
and the one who seeks, finds;
and to the one who knocks,
the door will be opened.

Mt. 7:7-8

I tell you,
all that you ask for in prayer,
believe that you will receive it
and it shall be yours.

Mk. 11:24

Correct me, Lord, but with care,
not in anger, lest you bring me to nothing.

Jer. 10:24

CONFIDENCE IN GOD

Come to me,
all you who labor and are burdened,
and I will give you rest.
Take my yoke upon you
and learn from me,
for I am meek and humble of heart;
and you will find rest for yourselves.
for my yoke is easy and my burden light.

Mt. 11: 28-30

My grace is sufficient for you,
for power is made perfect in weakness.

2 Cor. 12:9

Do not worry about tomorrow;
tomorrow will take care of itself.
Sufficient for a day is its own evil.

Mt. 6:34

If God so clothes the grass of the field,
which grows today and tomorrow is thrown
into the oven, will he not much more provide
for you, O you of little faith?

Mt. 6:30

Study the generations gone by
and ask yourself:
Has anyone hoped in the Lord
and been disappointed?
Has anyone done all he could
and been forsaken?
Has anyone called on God
and been refused?

Sir. 2:10

CHOOSING WHAT MATTERS

Whoever wishes to come after me
must deny himself,
take up his cross,
and follow me.
For whoever wishes to save his life
will lose it,
and whoever loses his life for my sake
will find it.

Mt. 16:24-25

What profit would there be for you
to gain the whole world
and lose your own life?

Mt. 16:26

Fight for truth to the death
and God will battle at your side.

Sr. 28

FRIENDSHIP

Be careful when you look for a friend,
for one sort of friend
is a friend when it suits him,
when you need him, he will not be there.
Another friend can turn into your enemy,
and only bring you shame.
Another friend, a boon companion,
will not be at your side in sorrow,
then he avoids you.
A faithful friend, though, is a sturdy shelter,
a treasure when he is found.
A faithful friend is beyond price,
no sum can measure his worth.
A faithful friend forever brings you life.

Sir. 6:7-16

Jesus said to His disciples:
"This My commandment:
love one another
as I have loved you.
There is no greater love than this:
to lay down one's life for one's friends.
You are My friends
if you do what I command you.
I no longer speak of you as slaves,
for a slave does not know
what his master is about.
Instead, I call you friends,
since I have made known to you
all that I heard from My Father.
It was not you who chose me,
it was I who chose you
to go forth and bear fruit."

Jn. 15: 12-15

The World to Come

Behold I am coming soon.
I bring with Me the recompense
I will give to each according to his deeds.

Rev. 22:12

Do not let your hearts be troubled.
You have faith in God;
have faith in Me also.
In My Father's house there are
many dwelling places;
otherwise how could I have told you
that I was going to prepare a place for you?
I am indeed going to prepare a place for you
and then I shall come back
to take you with Me,
that where I am you also may be.

Jn. 14: 1-4

See what love the Father has bestowed on us
that we may be called the children of God.
Yet so we are.

I Jn. 3:1

MAY
THE PASSION
OF
JESUS CHRIST
BE EVER
IN
YOUR HEARTS